VOYAGE TO THE SUN
The Tao te Ching for Children

Written by Ruth Oskolkoff
Illustrated by Joan Hunter Iovino

Copyright © 2015 Ruth Ann Oskolkoff

All rights reserved.

ISBN-13: 978-1512244397
ISBN-10: 1512244392

DEDICATION

For Dee Brown, a mother and a beautiful human being. Glad you are my friend.

CONTENTS

ACKNOWLEDGMENTS...................i
WHO IS LA-SING? 1
THE WORD T-A-O.......................4
WATER IN A CUP 6
LEARNING TO HEAR 8
THE STAR STUDENT....................10
WHERE IS THE TAO? 12
BECOMING A CLEAR POOL...........14
THE JOURNEY OF THOUGHTS......16
WHAT IS MAGIC? 18
THE CHILD WHO TOUCHES
THE WHOLE WORLD....................20
WHAT IS REAL? 22
ALL PEOPLE...............................24
HOW TO ORGANIZE 26
THE VOYAGE TO THE SUN 28
LA-SING IS CURIOUS...................30
THE BIG CITIES..........................32
TEACHERS 34
THE SMART GARDENER 36
THREE THINGS 38

ACKNOWLEDGMENTS

I acknowledge those who have already written a version of the Tao.
I looked around for a children's version so I could read it to my son.
Not finding one, I tasked myself with creating a version.
As everyone knows, ideas cannot be copyrighted but words can.
What I have added is unique language especially for children.

I acknowledge my husband, who encourages me every day,
and exemplifies the Tao in many ways. He is the flowing water,
the patience of time, and the love of a good parent.

WHO IS LA-SING?

Some time ago in a small town
a beautiful elderly woman
who wore a flowing silk kaftan
came to visit the parents
of two curious children.
Her name was La-Sing.

Her voice was soft like a song.

The family sat in the garden
beside the mint plants and old statue.
The adults drank Oolong tea
and the children had lemonade.

La-Sing had been to far-off places,
seen war and peace,
studied unusual things,
made lots of friends.

La-Sing and the children
sipped their tea
in the beautiful garden,
talking of ordinary things.

This is their story.

WHAT DOES THE WORD TAO MEAN?

The story of the Tao which
La-Sing spoke of
is only part of the real story.
The word spelled T-A-O
is very difficult to understand
as it has many meanings.

She said: Once you learn the word Tao,
that is just the beginning.
The Tao is about mysteries,
things people cannot figure out
because they are trapped in their mind.

When you become calm and unworried,
when you do not want so many things,
you will begin to understand.

WATER IN A CUP

Being good is to become like water in a cup.
Water spills out everywhere but goes into any container.
All the plants grow because of water and people need water to live.
Water is in many places, even locations people do not want to go.
The Tao is like the rain, the rivers, and the ocean.

La-Sing said: Let me help you understand.
Here are some things that will help you know.

When you go to find a place to live,
live near the ground so you can garden.
Watch the plants. See what is happening outside.
Be close to the people on the street.
When you see fights, try to stand back and think.
Try to figure out if one person is bullying and mean.

In school and home, try to figure out what you really like.
What kind of toys do you think are fun?
What kind of hobbies will you have?
Find time for what really interests you.
When you are yourself and realize you are just fine,
others will think that, too.

LEARNING TO HEAR

A lot of bright colors
make it so you cannot see
tiny patterns and designs.

A lot of loud sounds
make it so you cannot hear
things that are quiet and magical.

A lot of spicy foods
make it so you cannot enjoy everyday foods
like bread, rice, and pasta.

THE STAR STUDENT

La-Sing said: The star student
thinks about everything.

She first listens at school, and
does what her teachers say.
Then after that she goes and figures out
right and wrong for herself.

The star student tries to watch
things come and go.
She lets her heart be open
like a summer day
when the sky is clear and blue.

The star student is like the sky.

WHERE IS THE TAO?

If you look for it, you cannot see it.
If you listen, you will not be able to hear it.
If you try to hold it, you cannot even touch it.

Why would that be?
It does not make any sense!

Because even though the Tao exists in the sky,
the Tao is not a bright star.
Even though the Tao exists in the deep earth,
the Tao is not the dark.

The Tao is everywhere,
yet most people do not see it.
It looks like nothing.
The Tao is hard to see;
it is tricky to try to understand.

Sometimes it is better just to relax:
do your schoolwork,
listen to your parents,
be nice to others,
and have fun with your friends.

BECOMING A CLEAR POOL

La-Sing walked over to the lantern,
her silk robes flowing.
She told us: A long time ago
great teachers talked about ideas
that are boring to people today.
We cannot understand
what these teachers were trying to teach;
all we know is a few details, like how they dressed.

She continued:
These teachers from long ago
seemed as if they came from a better country;
they were just visiting the area.
They were like ice that melted,
ice that turned into water
which could fit into any container.

La-Sing turned to the two children:
Can you be like them,
be patient until the water becomes still,
until you can see through it?

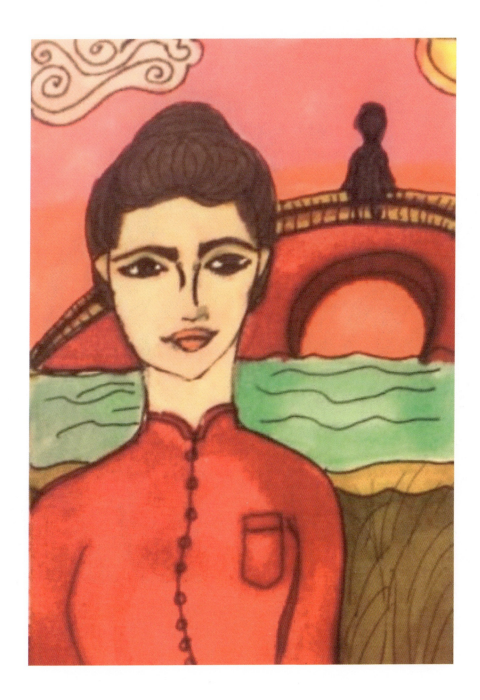

THE JOURNEY OF THOUGHTS

The father was inspired and put down his tea.
He told the family his thoughts. He said:
A good bus rider likes to take the bus,
looking out the window,
talking to others on the way.
The trip on the bus is fun;
it is not just about getting there.

A good painter tries to think about
What she is feeling inside
her imagination, her thoughts.
It is not just about painting
what something looks like.

A good science student
likes thinking about ideas,
tries to find out how things work.
It is not just about learning
one tiny piece of the universe.

WHAT IS MAGIC?

The mother walked over to the rose.
She said: The best child is the one
who talks to all the kids in his class.

He is polite to everyone;
he tries to be friends with everyone.

Students who are mean
need someone to be nice to them, too.
The nice children will show them
how they should behave.

That is what magic is.

THE CHILD WHO TOUCHES THE WHOLE WORLD

The little girl got up and looked at the mint plant.
A butterfly flew nearby and then fluttered away.
La-Sing continued talking in her sweet voice:
You children should know about laws,
learn about wars and rules.
That is okay.

Remember though, that imagination and love
are more important.
If you always hold to love and imagination,
if you can be like this,
the Tao will always be there for you.

You will always be magical.
You will be a hero.
You will influence everything.

WHAT IS REAL?

La-Sing sat down in a wicker chair and sipped her tea.
There was a slight breeze as she spoke quietly:

I am a dreamer.
I feel the universe coming from
the world of dreams and imagination.
We are like thoughts come to life.

The smartest people
know all the rules and facts,
but every day they feel
the real universe is like magic
living in our hearts.

ALL PEOPLE

We need peace so we can live good lives.
Children are required to go to school;
adults need to go to work.
Everyone must have a house to live in,
food so we can eat our meals.
We all want to be happy.

Some people see their enemies as only evil.
The great teacher does not see that
because all people have some good.

It is sad when mean people hurt others,
because everyone has a light in their spirit.
Everyone was once a little child.

HOW TO ORGANIZE

In school and at home
there are places for all your things;
everything has a name.
Your coat goes in a cubby at school.
You have your own desk and chair to use.

The wise child realizes
there are limits to organizing everything.
Sometimes it is better to stop;
just have fun and do as you like.

If a person goes too far
in organizing everything all of the time,
that is when common sense fails;
that is when real trouble happens.

THE VOYAGE TO THE SUN

Nature is complicated.
The trees, the wind, and the stars
are hard to understand.
The world is not always how it seems.

The walk across the street can seem long,
like walking across town.
Grown-ups with real magic
sometimes seem very ordinary.

If you know of anyone
who is a really good person,
they will probably seem imperfect
when you talk to them.

The best drawings are simple.
Special things can seem plain.
The voyage to the sun is inside you.

LA-SING IS CURIOUS

La-Sing asked the two children some questions.
She leaned forward and put down her tea.
She got a serious look on her face. She said:
Let me ask you three questions.

First, what is worth having?
Do you want to be popular with the other kids,
or do you want to do the right thing?
What if you had to choose?

Second, do you want to have all the best toys,
or do you want to spend some time
having fun with your friends and your family?
What if you could choose only one?

Third, I will ask you the hardest question.
Would you rather win a game
you play with your friends,
or would you rather lose?

What would happen if you win?
What would happen if you lose?

THE BIG CITIES

When a city is overrun with the Tao,
the buses run, adults go to interesting jobs,
children play in parks, and people garden.

When a city is not friends with the Tao
there are a lot of weapons and police,
mean people take over the government,
people get afraid and stay inside.

La-Sing said to be afraid is the biggest mistake.

No need to fight with other kids;
there are other ways to deal with mean kids.
If there is no way, sometimes it is better
to go somewhere else and leave.
It is sad to make an enemy.

Fear is like a shadow you see
from a passing car.
Fear is not real.

TEACHERS

The great teacher is not concerned with her own thoughts;
she cares about everyone and wants them to be well.

The great teacher is good to all the good children;
she is also good to all the bad children.

The great teacher wants to be good to everyone.
People just do not understand that, but it is true.

The great teacher is kind to everyone,
just as if she is everyone's mother.

THE SMART GARDENER

La-Sing pointed at the garden and spoke:
You can learn a lot from the garden.
The plant that has been in the same place
for a while will keep growing.

The new plant you just put in the garden
can be moved with hardly any work.
If a branch of the tree is dry,
you can usually break it with no effort.
Tiny little seeds are easy
to plant all over the garden
because they are so small.

The smart gardener
tries to work with the natural
conditions of the garden.
Otherwise the work is a struggle,
sometimes even impossible.

THREE THINGS

La-Sing, the elegant lady, stood up
to go look at a butterfly on a flower.
She said she had three things
she wanted us to know.

One, try to understand what is natural:
the birds, the trees, growing up, learning,
fun with your family and friends.

Two, try to be patient with everyone,
even when they are angry or yell.

Three, practice compassion with everyone,
be understanding and kind,
even if you are the only one who is.

ABOUT THE AUTHOR AND ILLUSTRATOR

Ruth Ann Oskolkoff possesses a Master of Arts in Humanities and a Certificate in Poetry Writing. She has studied many religions, has a few hobbies and is a wife and mother. This qualifies her to write children's books, comment on popular culture, and travel on pilgrimages. She shares an apartment with her family, and lives without a car in a big city.

Joan Hunter Iovino was born in Washington, D.C. and after a decade of travels across the United States, now resides in rural Maryland with her "road cat" Driftwood. She spends the majority of her time in her studio drinking cold coffee and making a mess.

Printed in Poland
by Amazon Fulfillment
Poland Sp. z o.o., Wrocław